# A Mouse

# in the

# Corner

# Poems by Dorothy Will Simon

### Illustrations by Patricia Holston

Exposition Press • New York

**To my *Three Musketeers*—
Si, Lee, and John**

FIRST EDITION

Copyright, 1955, by Dorothy Will Simon
*All rights reserved, including the right of
reproduction in whole or in part in any form*
Published by the Exposition Press Inc.
386 Fourth Avenue, New York 16, N. Y.
Manufactured in the United States of America

Library of Congress catalog card number: 55-11134

# *Preface*

This small volume evolved because of the often heard comment, "How I'd like to have been a mouse in the corner when that happened!" With that in mind, this has been written so that you, along with our little friend, are in a position to observe intimate moments in the home, or in buildings about the town, with the understanding, wisdom, and sense of humor which we know you possess.

These verses seemed the best medium through which, under the present circumstances, our kindly, sympathetic little Mouse in the Corner could share with you his experiences.

We hope that you will find some chuckles, a bit of beauty, and a key or three to memory's door between the covers—as well as our best wishes for a happier, more charitable world for everyone.

D.W.S.

Perhaps I should add that any resemblance to persons living or dead is purely a matter of your own imagination.

By the way, the Mouse says that he, personally, has decided that, in the future, he intends to think twice before "squeaking"!

*Evanston, Illinois*
*September, 1955*

# Acknowledgments

In this limited space it is impossible to name all those to whom I feel a very real debt of gratitude. Only because of their inspiration, aid and advice was *A Mouse in the Corner* brought out for public view.

I must, however, mention a few individuals at least, whose constant, consistent interest and help during the past months have made it possible for our unobtrusive observer to share his experiences.

To these individuals, then, our heartfelt gratitude: to my husband, Clarence Turkle Simon, and our two sons, Lee and John; my mother, Edna Blake Will; to Emily Kimball Lilly, Lew and Alma Sarett, Dorothy Somers Hoehn, Margaret Shoemaker Kirby, Dorothy Cain Nash, Maurine Morgan Mitchell, Dorothy Roach Holston, Helen Lenehen Van Kirk, Edward Uhlan, and Leslie Carver (unofficial "godfather" of "The Mouse").

I wish to express my deep appreciation to the Chicago-North Shore Alumnae Chapter of Zeta Phi Eta and to the Evanston-North Shore Gamma Phi Beta Alumnae Chapter, and particularly to certain individual members of each.

# Contents

# *A Mouse in the Corner*

# Question

She showed a bowl of faultless line,
Of beauty richly wrought. Delight
At sight suffused my soul. "If mine—"
I yearned. 'Twas hid from sight.

His voice, enriched with rapture,
Liquid, lyric, reached celestial spheres,
Exalting all in soaring song.
"If I'd had—!" Silence met my ears.

Her puppy hurt, I helped. The child's
Warm words of gratefulness, caress,
Were comfort. Grieved, I thought, "Had I
Been given—!" Turned. Found emptiness.

Beseeching, bitter, "Why? I've tried!
While others—. Dost think less of me?"
God's centuries-saddened voice replied,
"Reflect, child. Could't be jealousy?"

# Morn-ful Mutterings

With dream-bedazed, sleep-sodden eyes
He gazed into the glass;
Rubbed ruefully his stubbly chin
And muttered, "I'll not pass
Inspection with this beard. It's SHAVE
Again, as on each morn.
If only once—! When I recall
My early years, I'm torn
Between amusement and chagrin
That to this, man is born.

"In youth I scanned and searched my chin
For every silken sprout
I could admire and show with pride—
With nonchalance point out
That now at last I was a man;
My beard—nine hairs—did show it!
I bought a razor, mentioned loud,
'With such growth, best I mow it!'

"Ah, well, time teaches truth: Don't push
Events: Too, why be slave
To each convention and invention?
Relax! Refuse to rush! I crave . . .
My gosh! That clock! My *train!* My SHAVE!"

# *Thou Shalt Not Kill*

"Thou Shalt Not Kill."
"Do this! Do that! Move! March!" I say.
"No, I've time for play today."
And regimented, ruled, denied,
Initiative—a leader—died.

"Thou Shalt Not Kill."

"Thou Shalt Not Kill."
"Sure, Dave, come over. Watch me play.
Takes brains and brawn. Jus' second. Hey!
That's mine. Scat! Now—Dave? So—I lied."
Ideals and hero-worship died.

"Thou Shalt Not Kill."

"Thou Shalt Not Kill."
"Oh, not again! That messy paint,
Smeared clay—your clothes—the walls! A saint
Would lose his patience. How I've tried!"
The light of genius flickered—died.

"Thou Shalt Not Kill."

# Death and Resurrection

"You've paid your fee!" Mephisto said,
And sneeringly left her for dead.
His jeer of triumph rose on high,
Resounded, echoed sky o'er sky,
To Peter, then Scribe for *The Book*
Who stopped pen—and with searching look
Stayed Mephistopheles in flight
To Hell. "Methinks, 'tis right.
To you, though, 'twill small comfort be.
Through painful payment
Magdalene's free."

# Embryonic Empire-builder

He's ferocious!
A killer!
And thirsty for blood—
A conqueror!
Hero!
Could hold back a flood!

He's precocious!
A thriller!
"Superman" in the bud—
For "Mom" and "Her,"
Nero
He'd "hack" into mud!

(As long as he's
Tucked away
Snug in his bed—
And all deeds
Of daring
Are those he's heard read!)

# Beauty Beseeched

Enchantment reigns!
Her spell is spun.
Star-studded skeins, freed from the sun,
Are woven, warp and woof with breeze
Of silk, and scent of blossom'd trees—
Laced lightly with love's lyric sighs,
Then tossed, frail fabric, to the skies
To catch on points of yon young moon.
Envelop all!
Enrapture! Grant
An eager earth this too-brief boon!

# *Housewife's Predicament*

"Elevate! And at once!" our dear medico said.
"Eight hours each day. Feet raised over the head."
He glared at those "reddish" and swollen, well, "kegs"
Which I'd always, till lately, considered my legs.

"But, Doctor," I plaintively tried to protest,
"The children, our guests, meals—" He cut off the rest.
"On your back! Feet up now!" And he stalked from the room,
Leaving me with my problem: my feet UP—or DOOM.

'Tis said, under stress, that some answer will come.
But, "Feet over the head!" Run a home? I felt numb.
I've pondered the problem. Sole solution's, I feel,
"Magic carpet to lie on—and wings on each heel!"

# *Entreaty*

Please, Love, hold long to your
   Hurt heart,
If you think best that we
   Should part,
Each angry accusation (which
   I rue)
I've found, soul-searched, was meant for me—
   Not you.

# Simple Solution

A *happy* life?
Each one must make it.
You can't manage?
Why not fake it?

Try this, lad;
Plan! Undertake it.
Soon—it's real—
Can't mistake it!

## The Tooth, the Whole Tooth, and Nothing But–

I have a question, dentist mine,
That's puzzled me for years.
Why is it when a toothache—sign
Of trouble, torment, tears—
Brings faltering feet and sagging spine
To your door, and my fears
Are firmly—I think—lashed in line,
That toothache disappears?

# A Boon

O Pain—exquisite torturer—
Despair and Desperation
Delight when you join ranks with them
To further preparation
For destruction. But this boon I beg:
Withhold your fire and sheathe your knife;
This night withdraw and leave the field!
If he must die, let Peace—not Strife—
Attend our separation!

## Modern Marvel

"*Oui*, please, Madame, you weel asseest?
I weesh to buy ze *cosmétiques*.
An' maybe cigarette an' book.
I need, *peut-être*, peens. I seek
Some soap—an' soda. You *do* try
To fill ze needs. An' zat ees why
I find your great, good *Amérique*
So fine. *Pardonnez-moi*, I cry!
Forgeev, Madame? I have not been

Too long in zees, your great countree.
To see such kindness, an' esprit
De corps (weeth grouch!), I find, to me,
Means much!

"*Oui*, M'am, from France I come,
T'ree mont's ago. No more to see
Rouen. *Mais oui*, Madame, I learn
To take zat w'at mus' be, eet ees *la vie!*
I like your cities, an' *les fêtes*.
Ze 'andsome *gentilhommes, mais oui!*
Admire your boulevards—an' yet
Of all ze marvelouse for me,
Zer ees one t'ing zat has me floor';
I am amaze' at w'at can be—
Ze sings I find in your DRUG store!"

# Boy Bomb

Ready?
Steady!
Mind serene?
Growing clatter,
Yells and chatter.
(Best to don a quiet mien!)
Whistles shrilling and instilling
Shudders in a less thick "dome!"
Bam! Slam! Bang! Clang! Zero Hour!
MOM! I'M HOME!

# *Obvious Observations*

### 1

For these small confections
They spoil their complexions!

### 2

With pâté foie gras
And many hors d'oeuvres
Each matronly figure
Shows many more curves!

## Cave Man Conquest

I wonder if the "Java Man"
Who ruled this sphere, we're told,
A million years or so ago,
When dragging to his cave—brave, bold,
A beast he'd beaten, ever showed
More pride of practiced deed well done,
Upon his face, before his band,
Than he, who, battered—butt of fun—
Confronting class, engrossed in theme,

Transported and in rapt report
Of anthropologists' details
Concerning fossils, bones—for sport
Was stopped. Watched winks, but faltered through,
"First 'Man.' Did he affect us?"
Then rallied to sly challenge, "Name?" with
"PITHECANTHROPUS ERECTUS!"

# *Irony*

Determined that each child possess
That chance I never had,
I sent Sam to the Sorbonne,
"Cézanne, the Second? Promise, Lad!"

I saw Sue sent to Wellesley,
Tutored, treated to the best.
Maneuvered neat! She met elite.
Was voted "The Best Dressed."

Now Sam is satisfied to paint
A wall, house, big billboard.
And Sue gives sewing lessons—
Something few small towns afford.

# Mirror Meditations

Yes, Logic must laugh long at Me,
Myself—well, also I.
All three of us can be such fools
It causes one to cry.
When She tells me, "You look divine!"
I ask Myself, "Now, why?"
I saw Myself in mirror glass
And Father heard me sigh,
"More wrinkles! What a figure! Hateful
Hair; it's all awry!
The hat's outmoded—skirt's too short."
Yet—She's not known to lie.

"Why can't I take kind compliments
To Me?" says Myself, "Why?"

# Fear Frustrated

Dread Terror took him by the throat,
Thrust throttling fingers deep. Remote,
Beyond all succor, muddled Mind
Refused to aid by clearing, find
In steady strength, cold logic, truth,
The force to free the desperate youth.
And paralyzing panic grew.

"Can I help, Son? You see, I knew.
Let's face the facts together, Lad.
No need for fear. No deed's that bad."

An ally! Aid! Night turned to day.
Cowed, coward, Terror slunk away.

# Fifteen-ager's Midnight Misery

He murmured I was marvelous,
Showed captivating *chic*,
Keen knowledge—that such *savoir-faire*
Made him, mere man, most meek.
He mentioned minor miracles—
My eyes and dimpled cheek.
We danced (divine!) and left to seek
The starlight—all alone.
And then— O Mother! Why'd he have
To say, "Child, how you've grown!"

# *Fickle Phillip*

To be with you,
Dear Dee, it's true,
Is often Paradise.

To feel your arms,
Enchanting charms,
I'd pay a pretty price.

But I confess:
For Kate's caress
I'd leave you in a trice!

# Blessed Benefiter

My sister's hands are amber cups held high
To catch the jewels
Of beauty's bounty, laughter, love,
For friends, till then, Fate's fools.

My sister's hands are silver rains at night.
In spirits gay
They lave parched leaves, refresh, revive,
Then swiftly slip away.

My sister's hands are lyric larks on wing,
Who, as they sing,
Enchant, assuage, dispel all doubt
That Death ends everything.

# *Philosophy*

A little less "take,"
A little more "give,"
Might be the answer to the question,
"Why live?"

A little less "sneer,"
A little more "smile,"
Might help to make life's work
Worth-while.

A little less "me,"
A little more "you,"
Will bring Christ closer,
Heaven, too.

# *Strategy*

I said "Please?"
He said "No!"
Tried to tease.
Heard, "No go."
Squeezed a tear,
To taunting, "Ho!"
With a jeer.
Hmm! Be it so!

He'll be home
At six-five flat.
How he'll moan,
Finding that
The cupboard's bare.
He'll learn (Rat!)
What I'd dare

*For that new hat!*

# Me an' de Devil

Me an' de Devil—
We got in a spat.
"Go 'way, Fella!" I sez.
"None o' that!
De Lord an' me
Got things to do
Dat ain't no int'rest
To de likes o' you!
   "So go 'way! Go 'way, Devil," I say.
   "Go 'way! Go 'way! You'se gonna pay;
   You cause too much trouble in d' world anyway,
   So go back home—an' stay!"

God wants men
To stop dis fight,
Dis "gibble-gabble, sass n' crabble"
Day an' night.
We gotta show
Dat it ain't no sin
To live like brothers
In spite of d' skin.
   "So go 'way! Go 'way, Devil," I say.
   "Go 'way! Go 'way! You'se gonna pay;
   You cause too much trouble in d' world anyway,
   So go back home—an' stay!"

"Dey's followin' you has
Got 'n axe to grind!

Dey love demselves first,
Dat you'll find. An'
Dey's 'feered d' Lord
Will say 'Skiddoo!'
'N' dey'll land in Hell
De same as you!

> "So go 'way! Go 'way, Devil," I say.
> "Go 'way! Go 'way! You'se gonna pay;
> You cause too much trouble in d' world anyway,
> So go back home—an' stay!"

"Dey knows dey's lost
Heaven 'n' pride,
Der selfishness hurts
Down inside. Ha!
Dey's really mad
At dem ownselves;
So dey cause trouble,
'N' then dey yells—
Dat it's gov'ment,
Taxes, prices, jobs!
'Fraid to talk 'less
Dey's in mobs! Ha!
Got no logic
Nor common sense,
Don' 'preciate what dey got!
Dey's so dense!

> "So go 'way! Go 'way, Devil" I say.
> "AH LOVES MAH FREEDOM!
> GONNA SEE DAT IT STAY!"

# Miseries Multiplied

I often wonder
(Sometimes cry)
What is the reason
That when I
Am too tired to cross "beensy" bumps,
Our Garry gets the mumps.

I do believe some
Fearful fates
Must seek to see when
Strain abates;
Then thwart sweet sleep (The wily weasels!)
By giving Grace the measles.

Though weary, I may
Change my mind.
I realize we
All should find
Within—strength, fortitude for shocks;
But right now *Sue's* sick. Chicken pox!

# Just Like Dad

The salesman watched them as they stood
Engaged in low but earnest speech.
Their lean, young bodies, forward bent,
Belied the age the world thought each
Must be, since gaze and thoughts were held
By shining objects men desired.
The salesman's mouth in humor curled—
A sudden whim by mischief sired
Made him address the two, "Well, men,
Have you decided which one's best?
Which 'lectric razor turns the trick—
Will shave you smoother than the rest?"

One stammered, "Well, I like that one—
The lines—the motor—well, it's great!
Though Larry here does not agree.
*He* thinks that this kind doesn't rate."

The second lad at this spoke up.
"Oh, no! For most men they're not bad.
But I prefer—" his brown eyes shone—
"A straight-edge razor—just like Dad!"

# Change of Attitude

Smug wee Lee
Unwittingly
Sat on a bee.
Rose instantly!
With wailing plea
He fled to me
To soothe his injured—
Dignity.

# Star-led

The Plain of Pain surrounded me—
And Anguish flicked me fiendishly.
Ahead lay crags to climb—surmount.
Of journeys there I had lost count.
I knew the tortuous trail ahead,
Bereft of blessings—where it led,
The pitfalls planned by devils' spawn—
Grim nights and days of fighting on.
"Oh, not again!" I cried. "Dear God,
I can't retrace that road I've trod!
I've lost all strength of mind and limb."
I slumped to earth. "My soul to Him—"
I had begun, when loud and clear
Came, "Mother! Can you help me here?
I know not which way I should go."
Distraught, I prayed for help, and lo—
In answer to my desperate plea
Love, Faith, and Courage came to me.
With them I struggled to my feet;
My child had needs that I must meet.
I stumbled forward, head held high,
My eyes, this time, upon the sky.

# Morning Sour-puss

Oh, come not near me, friend or foe,
If you do value life! Just go
To any haunt not near my den
Till hands of clock show after ten!

# Hospital Visitor

Psst! Meesa Sime, may I come in?
I be-a your visitor—no?
When they don' look, then I sneak up!
Today ees my day to go.
Yes, eet's verra nice-a that I go home.
To see my man Tony I'm glad.
But oh, Meesa Sime, eet's-a so pretta here,
To leave maka me leetla sad.

Oh, Doc's verra kind, though he blustra some—
Lak my Tony, sometimes he scold.
"Now, Meesa Moretti, you mus' get more rest!"
The Doc, he ees good—leetla old.
The nurses? So busy no canna help much.
But complaina would be verra bad!
For oh, Meesa Sime, eet's-a so pretta here,
To leave maka me leetla sad.

Oh, I want that I see my small Angelic
And Tessa and my beega Joe,
And Lotta. You see, I no more can have
Since they tak out—what makes it so.
They geeva thees test—they geeva that test—
(Mees Bunnelli won' b'lieve wat I had!)
Then, "Out eet must come!" they say. And eet did.
It was no so verra bad.
For oh, Meesa Sime, eet's-a so pretta here,
To leave maka me leetla sad.

Wat I mean by tha "pretta" you wanta to know?
Eet's so cleana, so white-a, so good!
All the place seem to sparkla, an' evra one helps.
Though don' tell—I no lika da food!

Meesa Sime, I have thought! I buy white paint an' scrub,
Fix-a home like thees place! Ees not bad?
For oh, Meesa Sime, eet's-a so pretta here,
To leave maka me verra sad!

# *Reward*

To "go that second mile," it seems,
Is difficult beyond one's dreams.
But, oh, the pleasure, when it's done,
On roads ahead with friends you've won.

# If I Must Go

If I must go and leave behind me
Precious pearls I'd longed to own,
Must cross that threshhold yet untrod,
Leave lingeringly those loved—alone,

I think that could I bear with me
A dream—one cherished memory,
I'd choose a moment when, perhaps, I'd
Eased an ache—let laughter free,

Or needed by a friend, stood by;
Had somehow helped—then I could die.

# Psychological Sally

"Frustrated! Frustrated!" With her tiny broom,
Sally set the rhythm as she strode from room to room.
"Frustrated! Frus—! Did you hear what I just said?
Mom, when you are sewing, do your ears pretend they're
      dead?"
Glancing up, I wondered if my mind could cope with this.
Each hour showered problems posed by Sal, our six-year
      "Miss."
"Frustrated? Did you say?" I snapped my thread for time.
"Now what exactly does that mean?" I paused. Bestreaked
      with grime,
Her brows were knit with interest. "Sal, I'd asked before
      I spoke,
If Life had really hampered me." I hoped to make a joke.
A twinkle crinkled Sally's nose. "I just heard my Aunt Pat
Shout that. And then—she really did—she 'squished' up
      her new hat!
But I believe," and wisdom warmed the eyes of our young elf,
"It's just another word to say you're sorry for yourself."

# *Too Late*

"Oh! what fools we mortals be!"
Consoles me not when, heedlessly,
With careless word or thoughtless deed,
I've hurt a loved one, needlessly.

# The Friend

Rough roads, wild winds, she gave no heed.
She came because she knew our need.
With healing hands she bathed my brow,
Placated pain, while telling how
Her fearless forebears blazed new trails.
My lads, entranced with wondrous tales,
Forgot their panic at our plight—
The creeping cold, the darkening night!

She managed men's chores cheerfully
Though pained herself by injury.
No word of her work left undone
Escaped her lips to worry one
Unduly sensitized. She just
Worked willingly, dispatched the dust,
Erased our needs, brought hope and cheer
To bridge the chasm caused by fear
Of sudden death, alone. At dawn,
Our palates pleased and water drawn,
She turned to go. Our gratitude
She spurned with jesting attitude—
But kindly; then with smile that blessed,
Caressed us all—she bade us rest.

Tear-blind, I once more tried to say
What filled our hearts. She'd slipped away.

# Viewpoint

She sat alone
And dropped a tear—
For no one came to bring her cheer.

She smiled—
Gave help to those hurt sore.
The World wore pathways to her door.


# Christmas Morning Mental Lapse

They say it happens every year.
With giggles they confide it
To any eager listening ear.
(They don't mean to deride it.)
When all are gathered 'round the tree,
Gay gifts heaped high beside it,
They turn to me. "That *special* one?"
I wilt. Where *did* I hide it?

# Three Stages

"Bang! bang!" barked his uncle,
Cocking thumb and finger three—
Our baby chortled, tumbled down,
And hugged his sides in glee.

"Bang! Bang!" barked our "sergeant"
As he led his ten-year-olds
Across imagined battle lines
To conquered foe's fox-holes.

"Bang! bang!" barked the mortars
As marines, ferociously,
Besieged Hill 5, and John, our son,
Entered Eternity.

# The Home-room Mother Visits School

"Hello, young man! And what's your name?
Oh, yes. Of course. I've met your mother
Once or twice. And don't you have a brown-eyed, slender
     older brother?
Now, what's your mother's first name, dear?
A shame! It's slipped my mind, you see.
No, Sweet! I don't mean 'Miss' or 'Mrs.'
What's she called by family?
That is, what does your daddy use?
I'm sure he doesn't say just, 'Hi!'
He calls her—what? How very sweet!
You say  he calls her 'Sweetie-Pie'."

When Jonathan returned from school,
Recounting exploits of the day,
He casually related what
The visiting mother'd had to say.
I beamed with pride, with glowing face
Told Dad, who only shook his head—
With maddening twinkle murmured this, "My dear,
Think what he *might* have said."

# This Hurts Me More
# Than It Does You!

"This hurts me more than it does you!"
I stated firmly as my shoe
Rapped sharply his behind.
                    What use?
For all the while I searched my mind
To see what error I could find
In teaching him
                    Life's truths.
And did I have to act the shrew?
Bemoan the day, and start, "Why you—!"
My tongue a
                    Demon loose?
As anger cooled, it came to me
That at his age I'd done as he,
And had much
                    Less abuse.
So when I said, "This hurts me more—"
My heart and conscience *did* hurt *sore!*
I'd erred—that phrase my
                    Poor excuse.

# *To My Husband*

Without your wisdom,
    Knowledge great—
Without your kindness,
    Scorning hate,
I'd not be near.

Without your hand
    To steady me,
To lighten burdens
    Thoughtfully,
I'd not be here.

Without your smile,
    Your steadfast love,
Your way of life
    Like His above—
I'd die, my dear!

# Current Constant Question

Could I but find a master mind,
I'd ask of him this riddle:
Why do we mortals live by "ads,"
And dance to fashion's fiddle?
Why hurry, skurry, shove, and worry,
Increase life's pace deliriously,
To have the most, of travel boast?
Worse—take ourselves so seriously!

# Query

To try to write like Ogden Nash
Might seem to most men bold and brash.
But why should he have all the fun of
Wielding words which there are none of?

# Family Retainer

Yas'm! Yas'm! No one's t' blame.
Cain't quite leave y'all, jest d' same!
Don' seem right jest t' let ya be
'Thout any help—one like me.

Yas'm! Yas'm! Ah hearn y' say
Ain't 'nuff money fer m' reg'lar pay.
But please, Mis' Lou, der's moah t' life
Den dollahs an' grabbin'. Too much strife
Is caus'd cuz mos' folks nowadays
F'get what's 'portant. An', anyways,
Ah likes some love 'n' kindness, an'
Some understandin' of the ways of man.
Ah likes mah livin' like de Lord did preach—
A helpin' an' a servin' in de way dat each
Kin do—de best his life will 'low.

'N' dat's why I'se so suah right now
Ah *cain't* leave y'all for this Mis' Seah.
Ah wants t' be happy—'n' *stay right heah!*

# Flippancy?

Frantic Fanny
"Flipped her lid!"
"Foolish!" frowned friends.
Still she did.
For when "Old Nick" stacks
Woe on woes—
Fillipp! You may be
Next. Who knows?

# *Continual Faux Pas*

Inevitably
Indubitably
With grave inscrutability
I'm asked by some official
For a card
I've lost! Debility?

## *Holiday Season*

Now is the time
Of
Contemplation
Perturbation
Vacillation
Hesitation
O'er choice for all of gifts—each one most meet.
Of
Invitation
Celebration
Mastication
Ulceration
From tempting, tasty treats for one to eat.

Of
Stimulation
Animation
Concentration
Consternation
When greeting old and new friends that you meet.
Of
Expectation
Exclamation
Explanation
Resignation
Induced by presents. (Aching head and feet!)
Of
Meditation
Supplication
Affirmation
Dedication
And prayers for future chances to repeat.

# Great-great-grandma's Christmas Reminiscence

My happiest Christmas? Well, my dears,
I must think back o'er years and years.
Time tantalizes memory's span,
And shadows, highlights when it can
Our moments of great joy or sorrow—
Perhaps to teach us that tomorrow
Is the day each one should meet.

Ah, yes! Now, what was it, my sweet?
Of course! My happiest Christmas. Well—
It might have been when my Aunt Nell
Gave me a doll with curly hair;
Or when my Grandpa built a chair
That just fit me. Though I see now
That as one lives—well, I avow—!

One Christmas Eve quite foolishly I grieved.
Misfortune'd hit. Hurt, I believed
We'd skip Christ's birthday. Then my Pa
Explained. Made plans. I think we saw
By making gifts from odds and ends,
All love-inspired, for family—friends,
What Christmas really means. Again

I recollect one Noël when
We rose at dawn, wrapped gifts and food:
Sang carols, and in merry mood,

With toys we'd made, a tree we'd trimmed,
Surprised some poor folks, eyes red-rimmed
From thoughts of their young ones' distress
At waking, finding emptiness
On Christmas morn. Our hearts were filled
At their great joy. At Church we spilled
Our gratitude to Him whose Son
Was born to show how Heaven's won.

I'm certain now, in all my living,
I felt most blest when I was giving!


# Christine's Christmas Grace

Dear You above
Who gives us love
And wealth of world incomparable—
Who offers all
The choice to fall
Or learn woes are surmountable.

May You again
Please teach all men
Life's not meant just to please us.
This Christmas show—
Help us to know—
Your gift divine—Lord Jesus!
                              *Amen.*

## *Knight Errant*

He stood apart, his cap in hand,
And nine years shrank to shorter span,
As stubby fingers, nervously,
Plucked cap and coat; and then as he
Eyed customers and clerk, he saw
One understanding smile. All awe
Left then, and courage conquered fear.
Squared shoulders back, he strode to her,

Gulped twice, grimaced, pled, "Please—I—Miss,—
I'd like to buy a blouse. And this
Is most important. It mus' be
One fastenin' in the front, for she
Has—trouble—tusslin' those which mus'
Be zipped in back. Though she won't fuss
If that's the way it is. What, Miss?
The fabric? Don't know that from—this!
Buttons? Hmm! Some pearls would do.
She wears 'm on her ears. 'N' you
Know things should match. One time she said,
I b'lieve, that 'taste and sense should wed.'
Yes, white, I think, 'cause it looks smart.
An' Dad said that his loving heart
Goes 'plink' when he sees next her hair
Some white 'doo-dads' she likes to wear.
No, that's too fancy. Th' other's fine.
It's nifty! An' won't give a sign
That she has trouble with that muscle.
Thank you, Miss. Now if I hustle
I can run and catch my bus.
I paid you right? The price—tax plus?
Y' know, this present's for my mother.
Birthday? No, just 'cause I love her!"